Life...

I got

a

frog?

by

PoeMarie

Life…I got a frog?

PoeMarie is the pen name for Paula Dawidowicz, a middle years single mother who writes poems that portray life, love, and who people are and could be—thoughts from what she sees, reads, experiences, and observes…

If you'd like to share your thoughts, she'd love to hear from you—you can contact her at poemarie@poemarie.com . Hope you enjoy!

This is an Artists' Corner Loft publication, 2013

ISBN 9780615786391

Cover art by ASDawidowicz.

Other work by ASDawidowicz can be found at www.artistscornerloft.com and
http://browse.deviantart.com/?qh=&section=&global=1&q=asdawidowicz

Cover layout and formatting by Kay Suzanne, whose artwork and writing can be found at www.kaysuzanne.com and www.artistscornerloft.com

Copyright for contents, 2012, PoeMarie

All rights reserved. No reprint or duplication without written express approval by the author.

Contents

The Longest Days	6
The Wedding	*8*
Butterflies	10
Frederick Douglass, Susan B. Anthony, and Me	*12*
To Kick the Bucket	14
Celebrating My Words	*14*
Differences	15
In Search of Fame	*16*
Walk Among Flowers	17
My Lines	*17*
In Company of the Great	18
In Search of Simplicity	*20*
Her Here to There	22
Stewardship	*24*
Life on the Ledge	26
A View of Nature	*28*
Sipping Tea with Nature	29
What's in an Answer?	*30*
Marionettes…	32
When?	*33*
Bridges of Love—A Song in Three Verses	34
How Now?	*36*
Light for the Soul	38
Simple Little Ditty—A Song to Warm the Heart	*39*
Aging	40
Friday Night	*42*
And Reality Spilled In…	44

The Bully's Deed	*45*
Nature's Kiss	45
Single Motherhood	*46*
Lost Loves	48
Charm	*50*
The Holiday Weekend	50
The Challenge	*52*
Poem Noir	53
It's Raining…It's Pouring…	*54*
Bad to the…	56
Another Week Gone	*57*
Another Day, Another…	58
Can't They All Be…?	*60*
The Play's the Thing…	62
Time Runs Away	*64*
Yawn…	66
Christmas Tree in June	*68*
Aspect Ratio	69
A Date of Birth…	*70*
Ten Days' Rest	72
Invictus Renewed	*74*
Take a Number, Please!	76
Ringing in My Ears	*78*
In the War for Freedom	79
Puppy and Kitty Envy	*80*
Hey Diddley Diddley?	82
Ghosts Spring Eternal	*83*
Drip Drip	84
Extinction	*86*

PoeMarie

Life...

I got

a

frog?

Life...I got a frog?

The Longest Days

Sitting on the edge
of the fountain, looking out
over rolling hills,

I wished that day had,
like the hills, rolled gently on,
bringing with it joy.

Instead, careening,
a raging stream, it swept our
lives into darkness.

Baseball cap, white van,
thwarted abduction attempt,
stalker unforeseen.

Exploding the next
day, born of almost was—tears,
paralyzing fear.

Walking wraithlike now,
conscious thought an enemy,
I pause, take a breath.

How to be strength a
daughter almost lost needs when
almosts rack my soul?

How to clutch hope tight
when images of such loss
unleash mindless fears?

By the fountain now,
the air feels clear, refreshing,
something to savor.

Here in a new place
away from home familiar,
the past feels erased.

But the man, still free,
poses no less threat today
than just days before.

Unfound, unseen, he
roams free, holding us hostage
to his liberty.

So, we hide ourselves
beyond reality's reach,
peace a distant dream.

The Wedding

He tuxedo dressed,
me in a flowing white gown,
anchor in his hands.

We spoke our I dos
and walked off to forever
to drown by wedlock.

Souls on the ocean
drift on a wave-battered boat
without our sea legs.

Desperate, we sought
a give and take, a rhythm
to sustain our love.

Sea legs never came.
Souls, slammed on rails, hearts bloodied,
drew shark swarms to us.

Then, a miracle!
Wave enveloped, our boat dropped
onto a sand bar.

Two water-logged hearts
stranded in a landlocked vale.
How could love survive?

We had hoped love would
explode inside us, burning
brightly forever.

Farmers, we nurtured
love's seeds once planted, and hoped
to sow fertile hearts.

But our seeds, denied
soil for so long, would not take
root. Our souls withered.

Love cannot survive
in sun-bleached, salt-poisoned soil.
One day it expired.

Resuscitation,
tried many times, transformed to
a strong dessicant.

What we had not reached
in marriage—to sail skyward—
we reached at its end.

Anchored hearts, become
dried dust lifted by the breeze,
we finally soared.

Butterflies

Some say butterflies'
Russian flutters collapse a
Spanish orphanage.

What ruin truly
befalls tortured lands if the
bright flutterers die?

With butterflies gone,
what other parts of Nature
would also collapse?

A holistic soul
once said that all of Nature
was found in one seed.

What of butterflies
who fertilize many seeds
in their wide travels?

Can the holism
of Nature survive without
one more seed spreader?

We answer bravely
with a loud, emphatic yes,
yet we answer wrong.

Silly human seeds
who pretend to dominate
a world uncontrolled!

Frederick Douglass,
Susan B. Anthony, and Me

We bang against the brick wall daily,
not with hammers, rams, or maces,
but with our heads' stubbornness,
teeth rattles shaking loose its mortar.

We bleed openly for others,
through good deeds and suffered abuse,
traipsing our lives out on display
like the unseen slaves we fight to free,

Knowing others will be mocked, abused,
knowing they will suffer by birth,
knowing we might never see change,
and if so, not of people's souls.

We Don Quixotes, hoping hearts will change,
our dreams impossible, lie to ourselves,
saying our dreams are only improbable,
not seeing beyond the blinders we've donned.

Cellophane-wrapped leaders clamor for footing
on a narrow, icy path, but find no toehold,
no haven from teeming masses straining to
remove oppressors' shields and rub shoulders.

We dreamers of improbable
would rip a hole in elite's wrappers,
yet what reflections wrappers hide
dreamers can only imagine.

We know abandoning the wall
fosters problems and weakens hope,
and only shared visions create
the map others may choose to follow.

And so we beat our unequal crowns
against the not yet crumbling wall,
gasping breaths and biting tongues, yet
hiding from harsh reality.

Life...I got a frog?

To Kick the Bucket

Deflated, decaying soul, crumpled yet hopeful,
praying this would soon be his deathbed.
Wife and children, attendant yet absent,
Scurried, created chaos, but remained bucketless.

An agonized, unheard croak—he could no longer kick;
begging for mercy, cursing bucket-ruling stars,
seeing now his eternity as a hollowed shell,
tortured, abandoned, future and past blurred to nothing.

Celebrating My Words...

Words, words, words, words on paper like images,
like thoughts and dreams and dreams of worlds,
words painting feelings both common and singular,
words, words, words.

Words, streaked in the air, bringing laughter
from my children, a joy I wrap around myself
to deflect negatives daily and warm me at night,
words, words, words.

Words as plays, words as jokes, words as thoughts
perhaps smart, perhaps glib, perhaps thoughtless.
Words as hopes, as messages, as stories, as life.
Words as windows to the soul.

Rumored vaccinated with a
phonograph needle at birth,
I celebrate myself—my mind,
my heart, my soul, my self—in words.

Differences

Cocooned in my home, sheltered from differences,
surrounded by my uniqueness, colorless yet colorful,
I contemplate dissimilarities—color, rhythm—
and console myself with my neutrality.

Yet, a war rages outside wooden doors,
and as outside penetrates permeable wood,
unavoidable, unchosen, unendorsed war enters,
with which I must grapple, even inside my walls.

So many shades, so much confusion,
colors and rhythms inherently beautiful
made ugly by difference, by di-stinc-tion,
as though stink could exist without corrupting.

Not beautiful but ugly becomes
the order of the day—not sameness,
but unsameness, failing to burst the cocoon,
decays to superiority and subjugation.

Oh, foolish mortals, who see the mirror cracked,
who focus on dominating those around them
to blur the edges of their own jagged natures
rather than gluing their errant shards back.

Still, 'til indeterminate humans determine
to mend not just cracks, but depths of their souls,
colors and rhythms, beautiful rarely to distincts,
may only prove sacred in cocoons like my own.

In Search of Fame

Fame—for everyone to know my name,
to sing my praises, those fools
with no goals, no commitment
who see me as prophet, soothsayer.

Never did I conceive such a role;
me, speaking only my beliefs,
often ignored, by my own abhorred,
in all the world no space my home.

What could I know of the future,
assuming it would be better
than my today, lessons learned and
Mankind egalitarian?

Still, my heart warms to discover
my words still hold their planned meaning
if humanity still struggles
against intransigent selfish wills.

So, if Humans still battle their nature,
I thank the stars I help with their fight.
And if my words inspire others,
Perhaps they'll manage to make the world right.

Walk Among Flowers

I walked all day long,
wandering among flowers.
It was refreshing.

My Lines

All the world's a stage,
and I'm a simple actress
who forgot her lines.

In Company of the Great

Here's your pablum, child, eat your fill
lest life reveal harsh truths to you.
You mustn't learn about hardships
while a guileless, innocent youth.

Perhaps reading literature's portraits
of a rosy world, gentle and mild,
will, like waving a magic wand,
remove all thoughts evil or wild.

Yet, giants face truth directly,
forging a battle plan for change,
drying out molded corruption,
shining light in shadows, on pain.

Their hearts tell them sand-buried heads
won't fight unfairnesses in life,
while those souls who walk through fires
open doors to diminish strife.

But what of corrupted mongers,
sensationalists who ply foul wares—
those whose poisoned truths corrupt us
and make filthy things bright and fair?

Would that they could become muted,
without corruption spewed sirens' songs,
without moments to use to subvert those
who without sway would become strong!

And who would discern who is what—
who corrupts and who enlightens?
Who would discern our human hearts,
to which purpose they are servants?

Weights tip on a hidden balance,
teetering once to and then fro,
hands tilt them when clarity slips,
battered hearts trying to grab hold

to some truth just beyond human reach,
guided by two powers that humans see
as dichotomous, yet to wizened
are the same harmonious dream.

Corruption exists in all human touch,
and so can the search for truth,
one goal—enlightened, uplifting change,
the other—the stench of cold, jaded youth.

To be banned for being the second
should bring to one dishonor and shame,
but banned for being like the first
puts one in company of the Great.

In Search of Simplicity

Surrounded by computer, iPad, television, DVDs,
as washing machine and dryer screech,
I walk to my indoor plumbed toilet and a
room scented by plastic-encased fresh breezes.

Air conditioning makes sterile, cool air,
a balm against the balmy air outside.
Water filter removes years of human
silt, as though it flowed down a mountain side.

My token—natural clothes made of cotton,
downy soft and fresh—cling to my lightly powdered skin,
kept soft and supple by collagen lotion.
With modern conveniences, I'm all in.

Oh, to return to days of yore
when humanity and nature were one.
Oh, to return to days of yore
when bugs and pestilence often won.

Oh, to return to days of yore—
do I really wish it so?
Simplify out the pamperings
that in this future of ours grow?

Thoreau had his Walden, his statement on the times.
Thoreau had his Walden, but was simplicity prime,
or was it separation from government corruption he sought,
nature or autonomy of solitude for which he fought?

Was he some misplaced mountain man,
or the first hippie instead?
What truly filled him with joy?
What made him cringe in dread?

Given the choice—no EM pulse
or other nightmare forced on me—
I leave Thoreau's back-to-nature
life to him as his type of peace.

Instead, I will fight for my own—
with all conveniences intact,
and work for a government controlled
and citizens' power given back.

Her Here to There

Once lord of all horizons,
its timber drafty, warped, rot falling,
its roots cracked, broken, crumbling,
inside lived a wondrous room

where treasures mystical, mythical,
fictional, historical, scientific abounded,
themselves magically filling shelves
that multiplied in a butterfly's breath

until shelves mated with stacks
from floor to ceiling, sometimes falling,
leaving a corner for one lone bed,
chair, desk, and me, keeper who swallowed

whole all her Papyrus-inspired friends contained.
Homer to Asimov, mind's eye dwarfed reality,
Prince of Foxes, and Canticle for Liebowitz—
the world expanded, beckoned her to explore.

Heyerdahl and Tremain evolved to
Gatsby, Rye Catchers, Rowed Canners,
to books of fish and fishers of men,
and humor bleak and light

and often ironic, tinged with Heyer
folded in to the keeper's taste.
Decades later, eyse ripened by experience,
dark tomes read overdrive empathy,

their words, silent killers,
stealing joy's whisper from her aging soul.
Three children grown, she, anchored, drowns daily
in facts, problems—and swims carefree nightly

in the pool her old friends filled with
adventure, mystery, laughter, love,
added to with stories she prays
to share before her days are done.

Stewardship

I see, said the blind man
I hear, said the deaf.
But neither saw the Nature
that God to Man bequest.

Systems to discover,
to be nurtured by Man,
ecosystems themselves teeming
since all Earth life began.

Balances to be weighed
lest one side tip a plate
and spill it, hapless, sending plagues
to all ends, small and great.

And yet, we throw coins at the plate,
bombing it from great heights.
We, powerful fleas on Nature's back,
we ever rush the night.

Do we see the world as those of old
who saw God's provident hand?
Is the problem lack of reverence?
Do we truly understand?

Perhaps today, we see the truth
that only with our aid
will Nature yet survive,
and only if we can make

others see the immutable
truth that, through time and space itself,
we bear responsibility.
God helps those who help themselves.

So when next you wander through
a dew-kissed field or spy a deer,
remember we are blessed by the sight
and hold that blessing near.

For, if we do not change today,
tomorrow is not promised.
God gave stewardship to Man,
but fleas He may not miss...

Life on the Ledge

Basking daily in the sun,
done by me for health and fun,
lying on the ledge all day,
scales changing from green to grey.

Once in a while a bug wanders by,
and I grab it, lady bug or fly,
my tongue darting quickly through air.
It catches the creature like a snare.

A shy, retiring soul am I,
skittish when others wander by,
especially those who call me game.
My reaction's always the same.

I streak away onto the brick wall,
or in a hole in the ground I crawl.
I'm glad I chose the brick wall instead
of the fence around the garden bed

where a few sharp grass blades explode
from parched, chemical-treated soil.
With quarry sparse to quench the thirst,
I might find my good luck reversed.

PoeMarie

My Uncle Sal told me the story
when he returned to this territory
shrunken, almost crisp, barely a breath.
He made me glad I'd never left.

Here, shutters shade me during the day
and give me needed quick getaways
when I wait seconds too long to dart
away from dangers. Be still my heart.

So small am I, a fear can kill.
But then, I can fake dead at will
by breaking off my tail to fool
predators who've caught me, a jewel.

One tail down, a new one grows on
to help me slither quietly on,
unseen by predators, prey—beyond
the touch of all things and everyone.

Basking daily on the sunny ledge,
living on nature's spindly edge,
hoping in the end for one more day
of moisture, sweet bugs, and warm sun's rays.

A View of Nature

We mortals wander far from whence we came.
We grasp at clouds and stars and shadows
of what we could force ourselves to be
and forget who we morph into naturally.

We nurture minds and mind nothing else.
We walk past beauty, grasping at shiny.
We talk of windmills, ignoring the wind.
We reach to be more, and decay to less.

Mortals may fly, but at what price—
the loss of soul, of breath, of wisdom,
to become jaded, hardened, determined,
no longer rosy, simple, childlike?

Man's answer—walking again with nature
instead of walking unseeing, unseen—
though seeming simple proves complex,
too complex for modern man, it seems.

Sipping Tea with Nature

Nature, another object on my shelf
like a book, a doll, or a melted chocolate
spat out by a tantrummed child,
yet screams unheard on Her own breeze.

I, ear pressed to glass on the bookcase edge,
struggle to hear Her muffled voice
as She struggles to hear mine so
our isolated mines can become we.

Perhaps, dusting Nature off—
she seated in overstuffed chair—
we two could parlay, find
our mutual eye to eye.

But first, I must bestow on Nature
a role, not object but equal,
to see Her face, to hear Her voice
rather than dust swirled in Her wake.

Nature, once ancestors' best friend
and still succor of human life,
must become once more friend, lover, confidante
in life's dance if We are to survive.

Seated, sipping tea, sharing stories like long
lost lovers, We might discover Harmony's
song, lest the wind become the last
whisper before We're swept into oblivion.

What's in an Answer?

Quantitative research looks at numbers,
using logic as emotion slumbers.
Determining through crisp, rigid crunching
what a certain group's experiencing.

Qualitative research attempts to mirror souls,
to see beyond numbers down rabbit holes
to share what people often deny,
often in voices they use to defy

the expected, hoped, imagined, possible.
Goal of both researches? Search for the plausible,
the unvarnished, unbiased, unrecognized, unseen,
found by objectively viewing what's been.

Unless you're epistemologically challenged
by positivism—absolutism—making determined
from one location apply to all others,
often without sparing time to bother

to discover whether one represents all,
or whether, instead, researchers drop the ball
by generalizing to people very different,
whose natures themselves are divergent.

Or unless you're epistemologically challenged
by humanism—differences real or imagined
that mean no person ever fits a mold
and people's stories constantly re-unfold

to allow re-creation, reinvention, rebirth.
Poor foolish optimist, You, looking for truth
from the learned, steeped in their own needs
to in their top lofty world succeed,

to gain fame, to be recognized,
publish enough to in Academe thrive,
regardless of content, of a study's value,
foregoing worth for volume. It's true.

So what if integrity, abandoned, alone,
dies in some dusty, forgotten tome?
The answer's the prize most people want.
Any answer will do, if typed in the right font.

Marionettes...

Marionette, strings tangling midair,
head bouncing, arms waving without control,
paint chipped, wood sagging, joints flopping—
Marionette, aged and worn, rotting from within.

Voices—loud, constant—talk past it,
blaming, grousing, deflecting failure,
vilifying age spot chips, frayed strings,
as though stated lies change reality.

The trick—turn up the sound
'til echoes bounce off walls
and dins are all that can be heard.
Then what else can be believed?

Modern marionettes, plastic, paintless,
wax flossed strings, new joint systems,
gloss without substance, mega-mp3 and stereo,
shiny baubles, easy distractions,

accomplishing little, asking for much,
leisure the watch word and hard work a myth,
they mark their time as me instead of we
and least instead of best.

Decay surrounds us, piled higher daily,
marionettes beachside rather than toiling.
Disaster courts, dead flowers in hand, and
one wonders why old marionettes sag.

When?

When is too old to change a career?
When is too old to find one's voice?
When is too old to reach for bliss?
When is too old while still alive?

In my teens, I, a victim, suffered life.
In my twenties, I thought to conquer it.
In my thirties, I nurtured others' lives.
In my forties, I regretted young life's foolishness.

Now, in my fifties, white hair at temples,
wrinkled folds on face and unspoken places,
I sit contemplating my chances to find
the career's bliss I never knew I needed.

Who was it who sagely said
life is wasted on the young?
Who was it who peered into my
soul and knew I felt it so wasted?

When is too old to change careers?
I, still drawing breath,
finally realize no age
is too old to find oneself.

Bridges of Love—
A Song in Three Verses

Bridges tumbling, cliffsides crumbling, our world plummeting,
that's what will happen without you here.
Magpies chattering, my world shattering
without you to make me glad I'm here.

Scientists would say you were my black hole,
sucking me into your universe,
me now a planet, swallowed up whole,
yours forever for better or worse.

Bridges tumbling, cliffsides crumbling, our world plummeting,
that's what will happen without you here.
Magpies chattering, my world shattering
without you to make me glad I'm here.

Romantics would say my mind's run away,
leaving me better for knowing you.
I have so much I would to them say,
happy yet sad at their small world view.

Bridges tumbling, cliffsides crumbling, our world plummeting,
that's what will happen without you here.
Magpies chattering, my world shattering
without you to make me glad I'm here.

My neighbors all admit I'm happy,
happier than they've ever seen me.
Sometimes they even find me sappy,
something they never thought I'd be.

Bridges tumbling, cliffsides crumbling, our world plummeting,
that's what will happen without you here.
Magpies chattering, my world shattering
without you to make me glad I'm here.

Bridges tumbling, cliffsides crumbling, our world plummeting,
that's what will happen without you here.
Magpies chattering, my world shattering
without you to make me glad I'm here.

Life...I got a frog?

How Now?

How now, brown cow sitting on the fence
with a clown nose and elephant memory,
how does the guard-man grow
with tinkley bells and angeled eyes?

Peter Piper spent a year pecking
at pickled peppers with rainbow shoes,
wondering whether baby's blues were
afraid of the dark or of long walks on the beach.

Where did Peter pick his nose,
and why did frogs jump lazy fences?
When did cuckoos jump from their nests,
and who told Jack his beanstalk fell?

Does the brown cow not make sense?
Don't worry, there's really no fence,
and peppers are not worth a pence,
but Jack's beanstalk was quite dense.

Light for the Soul

Light spears from the sky
as rain pelts the ground below
and mud droplets bounce.

Dry parched earth cries out
to the clouds above, sponging
up every drop.

Dry parched soul cries out,
but no love droplets soak it.
It shrivels and dies.

What compassion spears
can human hearts shower down
on dried, crying souls?

Light spears from the sky.
The ground's drought finally ends.
Human drought lives on.

Simple Little Ditty—
A Song to Warm the Heart

It's a simple little ditty
made to be no more than pretty,
maybe just a little witty—
just a pretty little ditty.

When I sing it, I want to make
laughter, make you quiver and shake—
just a ditty designed to break
you down to laughter, jiggle and shake—

a ditty that can make you smile,
make you smile all the while
you anticipate the wild child
you'll become with the ditty smile.

It's a simple little ditty
made to be no more than pretty,
maybe just a little witty—
just a pretty little ditty.

It is just a simple ditty
simple, pretty little ditty,
falling short, I guess, of witty,
this small, simple, little ditty.

Did it make you smile, smile, smile, smile?
Did it make you laugh a little?
Did it make your heart skip a beat,
your pearly whites shine just a bit?

It's a simple little ditty
made to be no more than pretty…
maybe just a little witty—
just a pretty little ditty.

Life...I got a frog?

Aging

Back aching, she persisted.
Walk, talk, walk, smile, they insisted.
Oh, how she wanted to talk, share.
Oh, how she hated that she cared

about how she looked and what they thought
of the ideas she had brought,
and that she wanted to walk, enjoy
yet felt only throbbing, pained joints.

When had she grown fragile, insecure?
Was her star waning before its time?
She recalled how she'd chosen to be
a happy mother rather than thin, ogre-y.

And if that meant a life shorter
but adjusted children lived on,
She still did not regret her choice,
but hoped that time would grant her grace...

Too much to think, write, speak, and share—
so little time, yet so much there.
Words wafting from another's mouth
entered her brain, restructured, ran south

to remold to different concepts.
She needed to share where they lept, but
would she trust herself? Would time grant
moments to hear, process, foment, so that

all she had and could be was set free?
She prayed her moments would be well spent—
every second that she was sent—letting
her end become another's beginning.

Friday Night

It's a Friday night,
a very strange time to write,
strange but somehow right.

A habit once birthed,
with elemental self worth,
that brings joy and mirth:

life's breath to liver,
a warm blanket to giver,
and readers' river,

flowing steadily,
carrying them on swiftly
toward life's jetty,

capturing dreams paved,
storyteller's escapades—
the eves of Fridays.

It's a Friday now,
and strangely solemn somehow.
Let night take a bow.

I'm off to laugh at
a movie, then go to bed
to dream peacefully!

And Reality Spilled In...

I woke to unhappy people—
why is reality full of unhappy people?
I hoped instead by day's end to be sleeping
with happy dreams while in my bed.

The sun burned and the birds shrilled—
a happy day's warmth and inherent thrill
were wished but yet didn't appear—
why can't days be what we want rather than fear?

Tomorrow will be better—must be inspiring
because today was a week's worth of tiring,
and staying positive grows ever more challenging
since I know problems are never ending.

What a day! What a world! Here's to a happier tomorrow!

The Bully's Deed

Gum, chewed, then spat out,
Lint wadded, covered in grime,
stuck in the girl's locks.

Nature's Kiss

Roses tease her face
as petals gently kiss lips
softened to a smile.

Life…I got a frog?

Single Motherhood

Threading four lives through a needle's eye,
sleepless hours holding ill children's heads,
juggling balls not even seen,
working to prepare children alone.

Role playing father while mother,
feeling each day's constant smother
under responsibility's weight
in a jungle with blurred terrain.

Animals wild and animals fierce—
teachers whose words and acts could pierce
a child's soul without pause, treat
being one-parented enough cause

to callously challenge, diminish
without knowing the cause of singleness
is to keep children from harm rather
than take the easy way—the norm.

As though my becoming single
brought them some threat, some shame,
perhaps because they chose the norm—
regardless of consequences.

How ironic those bleeding inside
should be forced to hide
lest they, vulnerable, be stabbed anew
by the false righteous few.

Someone once mentioned wearing others' shoes,
but many pinch, so few people do.
Yet, knowing they pinch, could people be kind
and recognize life won't allow rewinds

to correct errors large, small, in between,
so we must make the best of what's been
of where we're going, who we become,
and what we pass on to those we love

so that single mothers, unjudged, accepted,
could live in peace instead of dread
and know cures to their shortcomings
others will end up modeling.

Lost Loves

Memories floating just beyond reach,
pushed from a brain crowded with sadness;
love, once cherished, the center, the whole,
now smothered in a corner of her mind,
a blood drained husk all that's left.

Days of laughter and catching a dream,
long abandoned to capture another;
his embrace's imprint cold on her skin,
his love's warmth ripped from her heart,
outward pretense all that remains.

Cold fear's knots bind her to him, though
her skin crawls at his touch, hidden to all.
Honesty with herself denied even in her cage,
welded bar by bar through years' suffering.
Now her self-clipped wings latch her within.

Soul parched, eyes fixed downcast, shoulders
permanently slouched, shame seals her lips to
all who might give her comfort, her
cage's keys, a better life…a brighter
future rather than trapped past.

Pressure building, trapped inside, explodes.
Internal wound goes malignant, and
reality races death's peace for sway.
Thick blinders removed, she spies her
long-suffered soul in her daughter's eyes.

Why hadn't she been strong for her child?
Like a disease, her daughter had caught
accepted abuse, fears, impotence,
isolation, slow death. With her parting breath,
unknown strength bursts forth. "Don't be me—be brave!"

Was it too late, too little, too much?
Her soul begged closeness, met only distance.
Would her words change her daughter's life?
As immortal cold descended, fear gripped her—
would her cage, unlike her, stand the test of time?

Charm

Bauble on a bracelet,
cereal we eat,
coy, winning smile,
and oh, so much more.

The Holiday Weekend

Monday entered, musty and murky,
bringing with it fatigue and work.
Another week gone, a new one begins,
filled with the same noisy din.

Tuesday tiptoed in, letting us sleep,
not a great second day of the week,
to be late, have to rush,
lest the boss, angry, threaten job loss.

Wednesday proclaimed proudly the week's midpoint,
putting the rest of the week out of joint.
After all, argued they, wasn't work to be
to bring lowly workers to their knees?

Thursday thumped its walking stick,
making all watch their clocks tick.
How Thursday hated being a day
when people's goals were to get away.

Friday knew it was both loved and dreaded.
Sombrero on, it preferred to forget
and focus rather on the party ahead,
turning dread to anticipation instead.

Saturday slumbered as it entered the scene,
waking only those who liked to clean
or do chores on the day before the great rest,
the day that to many meant being their best.

Sunday passed, serene and sublime,
hoping stomachs didn't knot as time
ran short before people returned
to Monday, that chafed and burned.

Then came the surprise—a Sunday wannabee,
a holiday that set the world blissfully free.
Just a teaser, a moment before onset of remorse,
for Tuesday-Mondays are ten times worse.

The Challenge

A new day must have a new challenge,
something to make the blood race,
to make the mind spin, twist, and ping,
to make the skin tingle with life.

Yet, what challenge should it be—
one to see decades passed in decay
before I reach the goal and find
years' work's final success;

or one that will be but a whisper,
a moment to complete, and then a
moment longer to enjoy a sense
of winning, then on to a new challenge;

or maybe one in between—finished
in a few weeks, smiles and back pats
and a celebratory toast
when done before moving quickly on;

or perhaps several challenges—
one whisper, one normal voice, one shout—
one for a quick smile, one for a warm glow,
and one to win the lifelong race?

Now if I only knew what I wanted them to be…

Poem Noir

It was a *dark* and **stormy** night
when a *stranger* **rode** into town,
dressed in a *billowed* **coat**,
sporting a TEN GALLON HAT.

Two ₛᵢₓ ˢʰᵒᵒᵗᵉʳˢ *strapped* to HIS *hips*,
two **carbines** *protruding* his ˢᵃᵈdle,
two ***spurs*** ᵃdorₙᵢₙg his heels,
his two *slitted* **eyes** surveyed the *scene*.

"Where are your children?" he ground out,
"Where have you hidden them?" he menaced.
The *CROWD* QUIVERED, **fright** in their bones
rolling from THEM in *wave* ₐfₜₑᵣ *wave*.

Where had he come from? *Where would he go,*
that **man** whose **look** could FREEZE A FIRE,
whose *touch* could bring PASSERSBY death
that, having known it, they **would**

Tearfully, mothers OPENED their ***doors welcome?***
to let EVIL INCARNATE search,
and *grasped* **children** *to their* ᵇᵒˢᵒᵐˢ,
FIGHTING *WILDLY* as he **tore them *away*.**

JUST when it *seemed* there ʷᵃˢ ᴺᴼ hope,
the ᵐᵒᵒⁿ ˢʰᵒⁿᵉ through, **FULL** *on his* **form**,
and *in his hand* for ALL to *see*,
Easter eggs glowed–*red, blue, and green.*

It's Raining… It's Pouring…

Rain, why don't you go away?
I've too much work to do today
preparing my garden for when you
come to bring us more than dew.

Must you make me plant in mud
as forty days' rain turn it to sludge
where plants won't grow to feed my brood
who hourly beg me for food?

Must I become a brick maker,
kilning mud bricks by the acre,
because my land has no promise
when forty days of sun are missed?

Must I become a ferryman,
moving riders, growing back pain
as I, noodle armed, battle oars
caught in mud forever more?

Perhaps I should just move away,
taking my brood to tropics to play
where sun reigns king throughout the day
and visitors bask in sun's rays.

Perhaps I need an indoor trade,
keeping the books for a magistrate,
teaching others' children to read,
playing at sparkles, bangles, and beads.

Oh, look, there, out there peek bright rays!
Perhaps Rain's campaign to rule the day
with clouds of gray has come undone
and, weary, Rain decided to run!

Now, I can go and plant my seeds,
and in due time, my children feed,
and once again enjoy my craft
without taking a daily mud bath!

Bad to the...

Why do bad boys get the girl?
Why do good boys just get hurled?
Where's the reason in bad winning
while good stands by with heart stinging?

Some women, like Florence Nightingale,
try to fix wayward males.
Some women enjoy the excitement,
running away from time well spent.

But, for whichever reason they choose,
they can't escape the questions. Why lose?
Why believe your leopard will change spots
when most leopards clearly do not?

Why do bad boys get the girl?
Because bad boys rule the world.
When will it change so good boys reign?
When good girls decide they're done with pain.

Another Week Gone

Another week has come and gone,
another week completely done,
and I've much to finish before dawn,
if the week's goals are to be won.

In my head are words not yet written
and thoughts that are not yet bidden.
But the week's gone with them still hidden
and my mind will not stop spinning.

So, once again I carve an hour
each day to on papers pour
the thoughts, the words, and so much more
I don't yet know I have to share.

Another week has come and gone,
another week completely done,
and now I work daily at dawn
so that next week's goal will be won.

Another Day, Another…

It was just another day,
a day like any other,
a day of both ups and downs,
a day when trials abound.

It was just another day,
spent hearing angry voices,
spent fixing others' problems,
spent clutching the table's edge.

I was just another person,
just someone trying to survive,
just someone abhorring lies,
another person wondering why.

Oh, now I've done it, become so upset
I've prepositioned the stanza's end,
something literaries shouldn't do,
something that limits their street value.

The longer I write, the closer I move
toward being worth only what I get,
to giving critics hard evidence
my work's zenith has finally set.

Was it really just another day?
Or was it liberation day,
the day frustration broke me free
to see what life could really be?

Liberation day, let freedom ring,
quiet, loud, as I wander, doing,
unseen, living within, waiting
to, like Phoenix reborn, burst forth!

Life...I got a frog?

Can't They All Be...?

Can't they all be long weekends?
Can't they all hold extra rest?
Can't they all promise adventure
and mysteries at our behest?

Can't I get a longer break?
I've lived over fifty years...
Workers get more time off for more years worked.
Why not people for more years of life?

I could report to work on Monday,
determined to work quickly and well,
labor for six hours, then break.
What a difference two hours could make!

Can't they all be long weekends,
days rewarded for days survived,
those passing on before their time
sharing their hours with those left behind?

I could write a play with the hours.
It wouldn't take me all that long.
I could draw a world's masterpiece,
one that costs a pretty penny.

PoeMarie

I could train for a marathon,
I could climb the Matterhorn,
I could spend my time learning lore
and sharing it at story hours.

And when I hit sixty, I'd get
another two hours, working just four
for the same pay, just a tad less work,
just a tad more time, just a tad more.

And when I hit seventy,
I wouldn't need to retire.
I could simply relax and work
two hours, then discover the fire

that excites me daily, rather than
suffer as microseconds tick by,
holding me captive to their clutter
until I, life's energy spent, slumber.

Yes, I believe life should come with
extended vacations for surviving,
recognized by one and all and
paid to keep old codgers thriving!

Life...I got a frog?

The Play's the Thing...

How is a raven like a writing desk?
he quipped, trying hard to jest
lest someone view his inner soul
and expose his black heart's hole...

Why was the Hatter's life so bleak?
Was he lost down the rabbit's hole
trying to jump high enough to peak
something not as dark as coal,

or was Sir Raven his truest friend, he
nightly summoned by light-challenged wing,
with all hope decimated within
Sir's feathered, mite-infested folds?

Alas, Horatio, I knew…said he,
his eyes pinched against errant tears,
his desperate hopes for changing years
mocked by his rampant daily fears.

Was his soul wracked with searing pain,
or was it something he strove to feign
to hide the horror he wished to rain
down on those who were his life's bane?

What's in a play–comedy, tragedy,
truth, error, lies, a good story?
What's the purpose–entertainment,
amusement, or simply distraction?

The play's the thing, the world central
for writers grand and writers banal,
for hopeful men and hopeful gals,
the play's the thing I'll create now.

Life…I got a frog?

Time Runs Away

Time came out to play today,
shared with me some of itself,
and then ran quickly away,
leaving me alone to play.

Time, a fickle friend, whispers
its moments should be treasured,
but leaves moment-burning chores,
minutes I can't recover.

Like a cheat, time made me hope,
think that it would wink my way,
believe that it would help me cope
as it turned me from brown to gray.

Friends all aged so gracefully,
smiling as their years passed by
while I, driven by Tehuti,
wrote down each second faithfully.

Seconds grew to years, children
watching me suffer for my art,
trusting me and my vision,
dutifully filling their part

in my hopes, my dreams, my goals,
seeing my soft underbelly,
shown only to those souls I
trusted with my innermost self.

So, timid, I hid myself
behind Laughter's joke curtain
until Time came out to play
and proclaimed today my turn.

Life…I got a frog?

Yawn…

Yawn one, yawn two,
I need to untie my shoes.

Yawn three, yawn four,
I may sleep here on the floor.

Yawn five, yawn six,
Sleeping will give me a kick.

Yawn seven, yawn eight,
It really is quite, quite late.

Yawn nine, yawn ten,
I'm still awake, so I'll begin again.

Christmas Tree in June

The room's focal point
to all who know its meaning,
it stands blithely there,

not quite majestic,
not perfection as before,
but just as sturdy.

Its balls now askew,
still they glitter in the sun,
and its garland shines

As ever before.
Yet, its branches, showing gaps
once hidden, reveal

its meaning—beauty
grows only through challenges,
unlike perfection.

I realize now
how like humans is that tree—
inner beauty not

seen by the callous,
judged wrongly by passersby
as having no worth,

being out of touch,
unrealistic, unwise,
their own depths unplumbed.

Aspect Ratio

My views, your views, ours…
aspect ratios without
a television;

A future's portend,
a window to pasts ancient
and not so ancient,

cause for discords great
and discords small within the
same window of time.

Somewhere between my
sight and your sight is the truth,
yet none can spy it.

Being so steeped in
our own sides, we do not seek
each other's visions.

Aspect ratio,
focusing myopically
so we cannot see,

spawning wars, vengeance,
discord, sentencing humans
to cycles of grief.

How do we change them,
the constant repetitions
of despair and loss?

Perhaps, like humans
purchasing differently
aspected t.v.s,

we change our channels
lest aspects freeze, and human
futures remain sealed.

Life...I got a frog?

A Date of Birth...

What's in a birthday?
A remembered nudity
screaming life's entrance?

Cake, oh so much cake,
diabetes inducing,
icing coating it?

Presents, large and small,
gifts of hearts and wealth of souls,
shared so selflessly?

Day to recall dreams,
to envision the future,
actively decide

priorities for
the coming *undisclosed* years
left to accomplish

what remains undone—
plays, stories, and books galore,
funny, happy, sad,

pensive and brainless,
belly shaker, tear drainer,
trying to escape

from brain to paper,
whether theater or film,
or just bound covers?

I will make my list,
and like a second childhood
Santa, check it twice...

Paper rolls across
the floor. Oh, dear, I will need
a hundred years more!

Life…I got a frog?

Ten Days' Rest

*Ten days to recharge
    batteries drained dry by life,
 acid corroded.*

*Ten days of faces
     new, not seen, or long time missed,
 faces that birth smiles.*

*Ten days of late sleeps,
   exploring eyes' inner lids,
 searching them for cracks.*

*Ten days' leisured walks,
    Well, maybe not leisured, as
 I sweat toward good health…*

struggling against
    back and knees and other parts
falling off—what fun!

Ten days of typing,
    laughing at imaginings
I place on the screen...

of smudging colors
    on deep textured paper that
soaks up pictures I

have yet to foresee
    but that, maybe, will help me
turn my insides out.

Ten days of bliss as
    my dead stresses slough off and
I begin refreshed...

until stress must be sloughed again...

Life...I got a frog?

Invictus Renewed

Rudderless, I ride waves alone,
oldest of my siblings, daughter
charged at my mother's deathbed with
continued family closeness...

Failure a brick around my neck,
I drown on muted memories,
deaf hearts screaming isolation
as icy water fills my lungs

and hopes drift to a sandy grave.
Yet death lurked for each a lifetime
ago, vanquished by me, although
remembrance serves no purpose now.

I would sit down to tea with them,
my sisters who treat me as dead,
talk of life small and large, and learn
the joys and sadnesses they've had.

I would sit down and share my love.
Yet what words would mend deafened ears,
Soften the hardened tympanic
walls, heart lamps unwelcomed, unlit?

I would tell them of my children,
the budding artists and writers,
my oldest caught in a whirlpool
of confusion, floating, adrift.

I would tell them life's tug of war
means never slackening the tug
to gain survival, happiness,
that slackening yields only pain.

I would tell them our mom, model
of fighting against darkest dawns,
and our Amazonian female
heritage keep me going strong.

I would sit and break bread with them,
conducting dialysis on
all bad blood flowing between us,
so years of isolation end.

I would, in parting, hold them tight,
my love for them flowing from me,
sealing us forever more.
If they need me, nowhere's too far.

My mother's favorite poem,
Invictus, guides me through roughest
shoals, revised as years of bricks drag
me toward the impending cold.

Take a Number, Please!

Like other days,
the morning spun crazily,
pulled out of control

before my noon break.
Yet, I struggled on until,
at three, it happened.

The nervous breakdown
dancing at my eye's corner
for many a year

burst onto the stage.
I screamed *I've had it.* Yet I,
a lowly worker

was ushered lineward
to take a number before
I could split apart.

Stymied, I stood there,
twitched, scratched, drooled, and banged my head
on the nearby wall.

Yet, still I had to
stand, waiting for my turn to
break into pieces.

I stood, parts of me
chipping off, scattered, falling
onto others' feet,

brushed away quickly,
mixing with others' chipped parts,
people chip mountains

that combined might make
a new army of workers not
yet marred by days' frays.

I stood yet longer,
contriving to jump ahead—
intricate, evil

plans to achieve my
goal—a moment's respite when
I could take no more.

Time dragged. Finally,
depressed thin as paper, I
returned to my desk,

pieces still scattered.
All went unnoticed as I
completed my work.

That small part of me
waiting for service died that
day, while no one cared.

Ringing in My Ears

What's this ringing in my ears?
What's this ringing in my brain?
More discordant than singing,
this blasted, rotten ringing!

What's this pressure in my eyes,
pressure driving me to cry?
Oh, here comes another yawn!
They've been happening since dawn...

I think I must need to sleep.
I did get up quite early,
ringing, pressure, yawning...
the day has been quite draining...

In the War for Freedom

War lives outside my door each day,
wearing the mask of normalcy,
yet carrying hatred's sword,
brandishing it liberally.

Not even called unarmed conflict
is the warfare outside my door,
although its fighters' battle plans
mirror the most vicious war.

Labels, decisions—which stair on
the case—the bottom or the top?
Precooked lives, planned and canned by
The powerful—who are those *the*?

They dictate what I can be,
walling off possibilities,
attack dogs snarling, ready to
bite if I try to defy. Why?

And if I don't rein myself in,
bowing to the collective will,
bent knees will become broken back
as cord becomes tightening noose,

strangling all otherliness
from me, scrabbling free thinker.
What about me frightens them so
I must become their sacrifice?

Puppy and Kitty Envy

I wish I were a dog, lounging
around all day, digging muddy
holes, chasing and hunting moving
targets, licking random body parts.

I wish I were a kitty cat,
queen holding court all day long,
majestically deigning to rule
my kingdom whenever I wake.

Doggies and kitties pay no bills,
never sweat over a hot stove
or feel bosses peel back their fur—
bosses, yes, but fur peeling, no.

Their food delivered by platter,
their bed is laid for rest.
Now, how could even the blind miss
Kitties' lives are among the best?

PoeMarie

I could have a fuzzy nose,
twitching at will like Samantha,
and could lazily stretch my legs
without signs like *high blood pressure*

spoiling my long midday repose.
My usual scratch anywhere
would not label me as uncouth
to other neighborhood parents.

I could let the world revolve
around me and my perfection.
Sad no one now recognizes
my extreme magnificence.

I must admit that having a
master to me sounds dicey,
but perfect sample that I'd be,
royalty would demand me!

Life…I got a frog?

Hey Diddley Diddley?

Who gave that cat a fiddle?
Who wants to hear him play?
Not I who has to listen
to him all the long day!

Who told that child to recite
those horrid nursery rhymes,
said she was quite witty,
her manner loaded with charm?

What kind of name is diddley?
Did someone think it a prettily
played twist on a nursery rhyme?
Who has enough free time

to create diddlies,
to play at farce,
look for sillies, make
intelligence sparse?

Ghosts Spring Eternal

Boogeyman'll get you
if we don't cuddle tight.
But, don't worry. I'll make it right.

Banshees'll come for you
if you don't do your chores,
so you'd better do more.

Poltergeists attack, surround me,
but it's only t.v. tonight.
What a rush, and I'm still all right!

Circled around the campfire,
whose ghost outdoes the other?
I lose? What a bother!

Youthful fears and dreams live deep.
Human nature remains.
Old stories live again.

Life...I got a frog?

Drip Drip

Drip, drip, drip, drip, I heard the dripping sounds echo
in the living room, as though some water flowed.
Drip, drip, drip, drip, falling on the rooftop?
Echoing through my mind—oh, please make it stop!

Why drip incessantly, for what seemed hours on end,
blurring eyes and focus until my thoughts were spent?
Why lay waste to my quiet, my peaceful evening,
drip, drip, dripping until my brain did sting?

Was it torture Chinese style or another method bleak,
or was it the result of some wayward pipe's sudden break?
Drip, drip, drip, drip, I heard the sound echo
through the halls of my brain, drip, drip, drip, drip,
driving me insane.

Soon it would not matter from whence the drips had come,
soon it would not matter who had commenced the drum,
drip, drip, drip, drip, must I listen, where was silence?
Drip, drip, drip, drip, unseen drummer thrumming, violent.

What came after the thrumming drum?
What came after, my poor brain numb?
Drip, drip, drip, drip,
from whence did the drip come?

Was it revenge of some displeased plumber,
was it the flood come to wreck my slumber
with 90 days of drip, drip, dripping
'til my brain could take no more?

Drip, drip, drip, drip, I hardly saw the jacket,
drip, drip, as they slid in, drip, through my front door,
slipped it drip, drip, 'round my shoulders,
tied it drip, off, drip, before
I could wield the drill to stop
my drip, drip, brain forevermore.

Extinction

A breeze drifted on the Serengeti.
A whisper floated on that breeze.
A hand caressed by soft breeze's path
made whisperer wish to take words back.

Baked soil, parched earth, land of flies
and brush scrubbed plants, where animals
can find no solace from scorched sun
and man can find no whisper of comfort.

Just as hope retires, man,
Sun-dried husk, fears having drawn last breath.
Then, a flooding rain, great renewal, and
last breath becomes new strength instead.

Teeming humanity seeks labor daily—
sustenance, hope in their own Serengeti—
praying for renewing rain, rebirthing breath,
dying parched husks from humanity's greed.

Will indomitable humanity
discover a way to thrive despite great odds,
a great chain of bucket carriers,
delivering life renewing water?

Or will callous human overseers
draw themselves inward, protecting
their vulnerable souls at the expense of
those they label less worthy than themselves?

As seconds tick on, answers crystallize.
The problem, like all other abuses,
an oozing sore the privileged ignore,
hiding it instead behind a painted veil

like blindered horses to avoid seeing,
constructing great walls against its touch,
while we, less fortunate, help build their majesty
with sweat and blood, thankful we are not yet touched,

believing we are safe, are different,
deludedly holding the mighty will not
crush us when it suits them, we faithful dogs
who've never nipped our masters' hands.

From whence will the water come, and how much—
How much to save a husk-dried world?
Answers, shadowed within us, wait to break forth
when the truly sincere ask the questions.

Life...I got a frog?

www.ingramcontent.com/pod-product-compliance
Lightning Source LLC
Chambersburg PA
CBHW071323040426
42444CB00009B/2067